# Never Make an Uninformed Financial Decision Again

# Book 1 - Understanding Money

by Hayden Burrus

# Introduction

This book, <u>Understanding Money</u> is the first in my five part series on personal finance. The goal of this book is to begin to get you thinking about your attitudes and beliefs regarding the basics of personal finance: Money, earning, spending, saving, and investing. In thinking about these topics, you will begin to understand how your beliefs shape your financial behaviors for better or worse. This book is the foundation for all the information and discussion contained in the remaining four books on personal finance. These cover topics that you are almost sure to face in your life. Continue your journey through all five books and you'll be certain to **Never Make an Uninformed Financial Decision Again**.

**A Note to Readers**
Readers of early editions of this book series have suggested that this book is a good tool for discussion of money issues within the family, including children as young as 10 years old! I am happy to hear that. Family finances shouldn't be viewed as a dirty secret. Open discussion about money eliminates that perception and reduces family friction around money issues.

# Table of Contents

# Chapter 1 - What is Money?

My son, Skyler, is 4 years old[1]. He has just started to dip his toe into the waters of money management. For Christmas, he got a total of $60 from his family. He also has three financial tools – a piggy bank, a wallet, and a kids book about finance titled *Rock Brock and the Savings Shock* (written by Sheila Bair, former Chair of the FDIC). He's way ahead of the curve in terms of access to money education. Yet, in his 4 short years, he's taught his parents that they still have a lot to learn about what money is.

Let me get right to his book– it's a kids book about kids who have a grandpa that matches savings dollar for dollar every week during summer vacation. One kid saves, the other spends. At the end of the summer, one kid is rich, and the other has nothing but a few cheap toys. The book tells a great story about the virtues of thrift and saving. Except the book overstates the rewards. The kids are getting 100% interest per week!! They are getting rich in just one summer (or 15 minutes – the time it takes to read the story). Skyler likes the book, and we must have read it to him ten times. He hasn't spent a dollar yet.

Many of Skyler's playmates are in the other camp. At the school picnic, popcorn costs a dollar. Those kids

---

1 He's actually 10 now. I wrote this first chapter a while ago.

that don't have money in their pockets go running up to their parents and say "Can I have a dollar?", ten seconds later they still don't have any money in their pockets.

We all probably know too many adults that haven't progressed much further than Skyler and his playmates in their money knowledge. So basic money management is not a natural stage of development like walking and talking. It's more of a learned skill requiring many years of practice and effort-- like hitting a curveball. Yet it's way different from hitting a curveball. Except for professional baseball players, nobody has to learn how to hit a curveball if they don't want to.

Money sense – well that's a different story. The average household income in the US is approximately $50,000 per year. Each of us are decision makers on what to do with each and every one of these dollars. That means that over the course of each of our lifetimes, we'll be deciding how to manage about $3 million dollars ($50K per year for 60 years of adulthood). Money management is not something that we can avoid.

So what should lesson 1 about money be? We need to know what money is. We don't want to know what the finance textbook definition of money is, nor the money supply or M1, M2, M3, etc. We need to know what it really is, one that we can explain back to our four year olds. Once we know what money is, we are prepared to learn how to effectively manage that money.

Finance textbooks and the dictionary have their own definitions. Here's my definition for use in the real world:

Money is something that you can easily trade to almost anyone in exchange for something you want; money gives you no benefit on its own; and if you choose not to exchange it for anything now, you can exchange it for something later.

There's three parts to this definition:

Something you can easily trade to almost anyone -- Before the credit crisis most of us could go to any bank and borrow enough money to buy a house with just a signature. We all had money then. Wimpy from the Popeye cartoon felt he had money also when he said "I'll gladly pay you Tuesday for a hamburger today." (I don't know if he ever actually got the hamburger, but if he did then his promise was money.) Cash in your pocket is money. Except when it isn't. A $100 bill isn't easily traded for something of value at a street carnival. But carnival tickets are. A blank check signed by Bill Gates won't get you anywhere inside of county jail, but a couple packs of cigarettes may get you plenty of creature comforts. It seems that kids inherently understand this – they don't have any interest in money until the moment they see something they want to buy. For some reason, many of us forget this by the time we become adults.

Gives you no benefit on its own – This is the part of the definition of money that Skyler hasn't learned. His playmates know this part all too well. Money doesn't fill your belly when you are hungry, it doesn't keep you warm at night, and it is not a place to rest your head. The point here is that getting money is not the end goal, what you buy with it is the end goal. If one of your life goals is to have a million dollars, you are on the wrong track.

You can exchange it later—If you have cash in your pocket, or money in the bank you know this part of the definition at least to some extent. After all, there are countless things you can buy on any given day if you set your mind to it. There's an old movie called Brewster's Millions (starring Richard Pryor). In this movie, Brewster inherits $100 million from a long-lost eccentric relative with the caveat that he has to spend $1 million a day for 30 days in a row and end up penniless. Also, while he's spending the money, he can't tell a soul why he's spending the money. Brewster's efforts give him notoriety but his friends worry that he's gone crazy when they see his spending. They worry because they think that Brewster forgot this part of the definition of money.

Have you ever met someone who has a job, makes money, yet never seems to have any? These people don't understand this part of the definition of money. Data regarding our national savings rate and numerous surveys regarding our saving for retirement show that as a nation, we don't appreciate the value of savings well enough.

The three parts of the definition of money work together. Not understanding all of them simultaneously leads to bad money decisions. In thinking about these three parts it's easy to become aware of our own individual understanding of money. Understanding each of the parts of the definitions takes a different trajectory in life. You may learn one earlier, one later, and you may never learn one at all. It's easy to identify the parts of the money definition our friends and family have missed. It's more important to work on our own understanding of money. Is there any part of this definition that you act as if you don't know? Take a fresh look at how you manage money. Do your money behaviors suggest you are aware of all parts of the definition of money?

## Chapter 2 - "A Penny Here, a Penny There, It All Adds Up."

My mother gave me that financial advice more often than any other. Now with hindsight, it seems like she said it to me 10 times a day from birth until I moved out of the house. My mother's job as a nurse was the sole source of income for our New York City household. Money was always tight. There was never any money for luxuries, even small ones ("No, you can't get a soda-- find a water fountain.", "Don't turn on the air conditioner – it wastes energy.", "No, we won't order dessert-- we can have dessert at home.") However she always had money for necessities. Each year for my entire childhood she spent almost two months take home pay to send me to a private school because "you need a good education." Of course she never let me forget how expensive it was.

Whenever I wanted something that was a luxury, I'd follow up with "it's only a dollar."

"I don't have an extra dollar," she'd say without even thinking.

"It's just a little bit," apparently I was confident I knew a thing or two about money.

"A penny here, a penny there, it all adds up." Case closed. I was good at math, I couldn't argue with that.

(When I got older, I offered the teenage response "Yeah, it adds up to two cents." That response didn't get me anywhere.)

So what exactly does that philosophy mean? Over eighteen years of having that short conversation with my mom, I figured it out. It means that big ticket items are not the only think that can break the bank, the little items can too. Never make a purchase without considering – do I need it? now? Can I be happy with something similar, but less expensive?

Can that really make a difference in a person's finances? You bet! It can make all the difference in the world. Consider your spending right now. List the biggest spending items in the past month. You probably have a mortgage or rent payment, taxes, maybe a car payment, a school payment, and then hundreds or possibly even thousands of other spending items that you don't even think about and have lost track of. These spending items that you ignore are bigger than the spending items you pay attention to.

Consider this family's monthly cash flow:

| Income | | | |
|---|---|---|---|
| Gross Income | | | **10,000** |
| Income Taxes | | | 2,000 |
| Net Income | | | **8,000** |
| | | | |
| Expenses | | | |
| Mortgage, Taxes and Insurance | | | 2,000 |
| Car Payment | | | 500 |
| 401K Contribution | | | 500 |
| School payment | | | 500 |
| ???? Don't know / don't pay attention to (DPAT) | | | 4,500 |
| Total Expenses | | | **8,000** |

Their biggest expense item is for DPAT. You may have a similar looking spending profile. Those only 5 dollars more on the cable bill, or only one more night out to eat that we don't pay attention to can add up to the biggest expense item you control. Much of this expense can be cut out without any significant suffering at all. Take a few examples –

A coke at the soda machine is $2, two liters of soda in the back of the grocery store is $1.50. Can you wait until you get home to drink your soda?

Your phone bill says that you are paying $7 per month for "inside wire maintenance" and you don't even know what that is. Can you cancel that service?

Your cable TV bill is $100 per month and you hardly ever watch TV. Do you really need all those cable channels?

You go out to dinner twice a week with your family at $100 a shot. Could you buy some pizza and watch movies at home one of those nights?

You keep the air conditioner on during the day because you want to get home to a cool house in the summer. This raises your summer electric bill by $50. Can you make do with a house that doesn't get cool until 30 minutes after you get home?

You will spend $300 on your daughter's birthday party, but all she wants to do on her birthday is play with the doll she made out of a mitten at school. Do you really have to give her the $300 party?

You are making your family go to your brother's house for the weekend to watch your nephew's first football game. You thought it wouldn't cost that much because your brother is letting you stay for free. When you list all of the costs for your free visit, it turns out you will spend $1,000 on airfare, parking, drinks, and a dinner for your brother's family. Is it really worth it?

You pay for a cleaning service and lawn service twice a month, they each cost $75 a visit. Are you willing to clean your own house and mow your own lawn for $300 a month?

Do you need to go to Nordstrom, or will Target do just fine?

The list can go on and on. When you think about these expenses, you will decide that some of them are definitely worth it. If so, then go ahead and spend the money.

My mom had a very simple way of tracking and controlling DPAT. She just made it her business to know where all her money was going all the time. Every day she knew exactly how much money she had with her (almost all purchases were cash in those days). At any point in the day, she could tell you how much money she started out with, what she spent money on, and how much money she had left in her purse. Every so often she would stop in the middle of a shopping trip, look in her purse and say something like "I think someone stole some of my money. I only have twelve dollars left." Then she'd look up at the ceiling, quietly adding up her expenses and then say "Oh yes, that's about right." Mom was taking a moment to keep track of her DPAT. Tracking this item and knowing everything about it allowed her to minimize that expense. At the time it was kind of stressful, constantly being told that people were robbing us, but it's kind of funny in hindsight. It was also her very effective way of managing money to cover all of the necessities of our lives.

The point of this chapter is that you should think about all of your spending decisions for just a second before spending the money. If you can cut that DPAT spending item by just a little bit, you can put hundreds of dollars back in your pocket every month. If the family whose expenses were shown above cut out DPAT by just 10%, they'd save $450 per month. At the end of the year they'd magically have $5,400 more in their pockets. Where does that five grand come from? Well, as my mother used to say, "A penny here, a penny there, it all adds up." Mom, you were right.

# Chapter 3 - Introduction to Earning, Spending, Saving, Borrowing, and Windfalls

We are going to start at the very beginning and define some of these terms. Stay with me. I know you already know what they mean, but thinking about them again can help with financial decision making later.

Earning – Money someone else gives you in exchange for delivering something of value to them. Working hard may or may not be an ingredient in earning money. It is a worthwhile effort to figure out how to create more value for others in the same amount of time. You can do this by working faster or delivering a more valuable service. It is also worthwhile to figure out how to deliver the result that others value in less time. It is not worthwhile to work longer hours just so you can tell your boss you have been working so hard so you deserve a raise.

Spending – Money that you have and willingly give to someone else in exchange for something you value. Make sure you value your purchase more than you value the time it took to earn the money you just spent. Make sure you value your purchase more than a purchase you might be able to make with the same amount of money in the future.

Saving – Money that you have not spent yet. Make sure you have some of this. There may be something you want or need to buy later.

Borrowing – Money that someone else gave you in exchange for your promise to pay them much more money later. What a bad deal for you! You should have saved money. You should have spent less. Shame on you. The only reason to borrow is for a sound investment that you expect will pay you more than you have to pay to your lender.

Windfalls – Unexpected money coming to you or going away from you. We like to think and hope and dream about a positive financial windfall such as an inheritance, lottery winnings, or an unexpected bonus. Windfalls just as often work the other way – job loss, unexpected health care costs, stolen car. You cannot plan on windfalls or create them, but you can be prepared to react to them. Preparation is easy – take your unexpected gains and save them. You won't miss the money. You weren't counting on it in the first place. Use your savings to get you out of the jam that your unexpected losses will create for you some time in the future.

Throughout our book series there are chapters on managing windfalls of different sizes. Later in this book we introduce the concept to you with the "What Would you Do with $100". In the later books we go through $1000, $100,000, $1,000,000, and "set for life". Windfalls are guaranteed to come about in your life. If you follow the guidance in these books, you'll be creating your own positive windfalls as you grow your wealth.

Investing – Investing is last because it is a combination of spending, saving, earning, and maybe even borrowing and windfalls. Investing is spending money on something that will earn money for you in the future. Investments earn more money than you spent on them. Examples are: an education in a skill that allows you to earn more money, a home that costs less to service than the amount you would have to pay in rent, a property that gives you rental income every month. Some examples of things that people think are investments but are not include: your car, the most expensive house you could afford, your baseball card collection, a degree or certificate that employers are not willing to pay you extra for, a vacant lot that you just know will become a shopping mall some day. More on investments in a later chapter.

# Chapter 4 - How to Earn

Most people work for a business of some sort. Business make money when they deliver something of value to their customers. Quite possibly, their customers may be other businesses. If that is the case, then your business must help another business make money.

In order to earn money, do something that helps your employer make money. Your employer will give you some of that money. Don't fantasize that you'll get all of it. You'll get some of it. As little as possible, to be exact. Your employer will work to find the lesser of two amounts: 1) the smallest amount of money you'll accept and come back for more; or 2) the smallest amount of money someone else will accept to do the same thing as what you are doing. If you work for someone else, it is important that you maximize these amounts.

Earning can also involve delivering a service that someone else values. That someone else will pay you for it. People aren't dumb either, they pay as little as possible also. This "services" category is very broad – doctors, lawyers, maids, barbers, babysitters, plumbers, mechanics, etc. Maximizing your income with services is not related to the skill or effort required to deliver those services. It is only related to the demand for your services.

Why do babysitters get paid less than lawyers? Is it because we hate babysitters and love lawyers so much? No. it's because there's lots of nice people who are willing to play with your cute child and are willing to accept very little money for it, while there is hardly anyone who enjoys spending several hours arguing with another lawyer about who should keep your coffee table after you get divorced. Also, you have to spend considerable time and expense learning to become a lawyer.

The best type of earning is the type of earning where you don't have to do any work at all. This is called an investment. Warren Buffet, one of the richest men alive, has focused his entire life on this type of earning. In interviews he often tells the story about when he was a teenager he bought a pinball machine and paid to put it in the local store. Others valued playing with the pinball machine he gave them access to and paid a quarter for the privilege. Young Warren kept some of the money and gave some to the store in exchange for letting him put the pinball machine there. He earned money and did hardly any work at all.

## Chapter 5 - How to Earn More

The most obvious way to help a business make more money is to do whatever you normally do for the business, just do more. A writer can write more articles, a house painter can paint more houses, a customer service agent can serve more customers. If you can figure out a way to do your job faster, then you are on the clearest path to delivering more value and potentially earning more money for yourself.

The next way is to do your job for a company that values your services more. If you have the skills to sell one hundred cars a month, you could provide your services to a used car dealer and sell one hundred $5000 cars each month or you could provide those same services and make the same level of effort to a BMW dealer and sell one hundred $50,000 cars per month. The BMW dealer will make more money from your services and will likely be willing to pay you more.

When I was a boy, a lot of my friends would go out on snow days and offer to shovel the snow away from cars so people could get to work. I thought that would be a good way to make money so I decided to try that in my neighborhood. I was disappointed to find out that I made so much less money than the kids who were shoveling snow in the wealthier parts of town. I thought that was so unfair because I worked just as hard as they did and besides, the kids who were making more money were already rich. Then one of my friends clued me in— next time just go to the wealthier parts of town to shovel snow. After all, they clearly value that service more. I didn't think it was fair for the people in my neighborhood. But economically it was definitely the right thing to do. Now I know to find the people who value my services the most and sell my services to them.

After you've maximized your value the best you can, you need to work the other side of the equation. You need to maximize the amount that your employer will pay for that value. If you remember back to the last chapter:

"Your employer will work to find the lesser of two amounts:

#1-- the smallest amount of money you'll accept and come back for more; or

#2-- the lowest amount of money someone else will accept to do the same thing."

For raising the amount of #1, first try the easiest method: ask for more. If you don't ask for it, you won't get it. When asking, work to convince your employer that without more pay, you will soon stop working for that employer. If your employer believes you and values your work, you've got a good shot at getting a raise. When your employer is deciding on whether to give you that raise, it will be related to the hard, cold facts of the real world. If you have no money, and no other job prospects, then your employer will know that you will be willing to accept just enough money to pay the bills even if you are delivering far more value to your employer. Make sure the facts line up in your favor.

So if the facts don't line up in your favor make sure your employer doesn't find out. Next, work to get out of that bind as quickly as possible. Work even harder so you can save some money. Also start working hard on looking for new job opportunities for yourself. Just because you are underpaid today, that doesn't mean you have to be underpaid for the rest of your life.

#1 is why lawyers get paid more than babysitters. Lawyers for the most part have lots of high paying job prospects and considerable savings. They will walk away from any job where they are not highly compensated. Babysitters generally have no other job prospects or job skills except maybe another babysitting opportunity; and they generally have no savings. Even though people greatly value the people caring for their children, they don't have to pay babysitters that much, in part because item #1 is very low for babysitters.

At the same time, you want to also be raising the amount in #2. If you can change what you do ever so slightly so that fewer people are able or willing to do what you do, then your income will increase. Here the most obvious example is differentiating yourself. Are you a wedding singer? Well, there are plenty of wedding singers out there. Your income will be limited to whatever your competition is willing to settle for. You want to become that great wedding singer that always thrills the crowd at every wedding you sing at. You want to be the wedding singer that people ask for by name. I remember one time many years ago, Alanis Morrisette sung at a wealthy person's wedding and was paid something like $100,000 for the job. Of course this is way more than other wedding singers get. But Alanis Morrisette wasn't being just a wedding singer that day. If so, she would have been paid much less. That day, she was performing the service of being "Alanis Morrisette, the wedding singer". She had no competition for her services, and item #2 for her was very high. (Probably it was also very high because of the large number of opportunities she had available. She would have walked away from the job unless she was very well compensated.)

## Chapter 6 - How to Spend

"Well, I know how to spend," you might say. "That's how I got into this mess in the first place." If you are in a financial mess, you don't know how to spend. You probably spend more than you earn. Most people are very bad spenders. They spend too much and buy things that don't improve their happiness at all. Let's go through two common spending philosophies:

<u>"I want that and I have the money to buy it. I'm buying it."</u> This is a bad philosophy arising out of lazy thinking. When you go to the Chinese Buffet for lunch, you don't fill your entire plate with the first food that you see even if it does look tasty. You look around to see if there is anything else that you want. Also, you may want to save some appetite for dinner. A person should use this same discipline with money.

Before you spend your money, decide if that is the best use of your money. Determine if it is possible to use that money in some other way to bring you even more happiness. Or it may be possible to get that same item somewhere else for less money.

Some examples:

You want a jet ski. It costs $10,000. You live in Maryland. Your best case scenario is that you will use it for about an hour at a time for each of 10 summer weekends per year. You're going to have to pay for insurance and maintenance of that jet ski as well costing about $200 per year. In 5 years you will probably be tired of your jet ski. My advice is don't buy the jet ski. You will get about 5 x 10 = 50 hours of enjoyment out of the jet ski at a cost of about $11000 ($10000 for the jet ski, and $1000 for maintenance). That jet ski is costing you $220 / hour plus the hassle factor of transporting it wherever you want to go. If you like riding a jet ski, save your $11000, use it to take an annual vacation to Ft. Lauderdale and go rent one for $100 on the beach. This will probably be way more fun.

You went to the movies and you are thirsty. A big gulp Coke at the movies costs $5. My advice is not to buy it. Go to the water fountain. Next time drink your Coke at home before the movie starts (or bring one hidden in your pocket). Do this twice and you've paid for a movie ticket. For me, seeing an extra movie is more enjoyable than a big gulp Coke at 2 movies.

You want a new Italian tile roof for your house. Every time you look at a roof like that on other people's houses you admire it. The roof costs $15K. The roof will last about 15 to 20 years before you need to replace it. My advice is to buy the roof. You are going to have that roof for at least 5,475 days (15 years x 365 days). Your $15K expense works out to $2.74 per day. It's probably worth it to spend $2.74 per day on something you enjoy.

Lastly, sometimes the people who think they have money don't really have any money at all. They have a credit card that has not yet been maxed out. These people charge their credit cards and never pay it off. They are accepting the obligation of paying 19% to 29% interest on the purchase. That means that the $100 pair of shoes are going to cost you $19 to $29 per year every year for the rest of your life or until you pay off the original $100. You'll be paying for that $100 pair of shoes long after those shoes have holes in them and are thrown in the garbage. This is obviously not a good spending decision.

Key takeaways:

- Don't buy something just because you have the money.
- Figure out if you can get substantially the same thing for less money.
- Figure out if there is something else that you would enjoy more that costs the same amount of money.
- Don't forget that the thing you want to buy might be in the future.

 "Most people I know have a nicer car than me. I am harder working, smarter, nicer, etc. than those people. I deserve a nicer car. I am getting a nicer car today." In short, this is the "keeping up with the Joneses" philosophy. There's several problems with this philosophy.

First, this philosophy is rooted in envy which is usually an unproductive emotion. More pragmatically, though, it is based on the belief that you want to be like most people. When it comes to spending, most people are fools. Roughly half of all Americans carry credit card debt. The average credit card debt for those Americans is over $7000. The average interest rate paid on credit card debt is approximately 17% per year. These people are paying roughly $1190 per year in interest ($7000 x 17% = $1190). Do you really want to be like these people? These people are flushing almost $100 each month down the toilet in interest payments.

Here's another scary statistic about many of the people that spend more than you think they deserve to spend. 36% of all Americans (and most people you know who make the same income as you and drive nicer cars) are not saving anything for retirement. They are hoping that Social Security will take care of them. I just went to the social security website and ran the numbers for both me and my wife. Our expected benefits are about 1/3 of our current income. I'd hate to not have any retirement savings; I'd hate to have to think about a 2/3 pay cut happening on the day I retire.

You don't want to be like most people. Most people are setting themselves up for a big financial fall down the line. You want to be the guy who spends less than what he earns and saves for retirement. A person who can save 15% of their income during a 40 year working career will have about 15x their income saved at the end of their career-- even after considering raises and inflation. That person can use that savings to generate a lifetime income of 60% to 75% of their pre-retirement income. That savings, combined with a modest social security check equal to 1/3 of your pre-retirement income, will keep your income stable even through your retirement years.

Now that's the situation I want to be in – keeping all of my money and avoiding $100 per month in credit card interest. I want to have my income increase from now until the end of time, even if it means that others may temporarily live a higher lifestyle than me. I'll gladly forgo a new car if it means that I can also forgo going down the dog food aisle when I am doing my dinner shopping after retirement.

Don't be like most people. Most people spend too much, get into too much debt, and are setting themselves up for a big fall. You don't need the fanciest car on the block.

Save your money. You'll be glad you did. In the future you also won't be like most people, you'll be able to spend far more.

## Chapter 7 - How to Make a Million Dollars Without Even Trying

We have all heard the claims and the ads. We've all known someone who seems to spend their whole life looking for a "million dollar idea".

"All I need is just one," a friend told me. "I'm going to find a million dollar idea, then I won't have to worry anymore." He's been telling me this since we were teenagers. I am sure you can guess how this story turns out. He's still looking for that million dollar idea.

Since we were teenagers, I've been responding "You can't make a million dollars without even trying. If you could, everyone would do it." The best way to make big money is by saving your money and investing wisely. It's been an endless debate -- my friend has had his big payday (and his "I told you so!" speech) right around the corner for over thirty years. I have not been indulging myself in such a ridiculous fantasy. I aimed to just go about my life and manage my finances without such lofty goals. Making a million dollars without even trying? That's for desperate and naive suckers who watch late night infomercials and respond to business opportunity signs posted on the side of the road. Then something very unexpected happened.

I made a million dollars without even trying, without even noticing, actually.

I regularly track all of my accounts on Quicken (a good idea). One month it dawned on me that because my net worth had grown to $1,000,000, I had made a million dollars. And I wasn't even trying. Now don't get me wrong, I wanted a million dollars, but I wasn't living my life with the goal of getting a million dollars, tomorrow. Yet one day "tomorrow" came.

So, now I know how you can make a million dollars without even trying. Go through your life. Do whatever you are good at and enjoy reasonably well. Then figure out how to get paid as much as possible for that. Buy whatever you need to buy to be happy. Then figure out how to spend as little as possible on that stuff. Don't take out loans on anything that won't appreciate in value. A mortgage and student loan are OK. Car loans and credit card loans are unacceptable.

Whatever you have left, invest. Don't make any stupid investments. Lower the expenses and fees on your investments as much as possible. Keep thinking and learning about how to improve your earning, spending, saving, and investing. See if you can save more than you did last year. See if you can earn more than you did last year. See if you can buy the same things as last year for less money. Repeat. One day, when you are not paying attention, the million dollars will be just sitting there looking back at you saying "That was fun. Do that again."

# Chapter 8 - What would You Do With $100?

Here's a fun thought experiment—Imagine looking at your bank statement and seeing a deposit from an unknown source for $100. As you wonder what you are going to do with your new riches, you get a call from Grandma: "You are so sweet, I put $100 in your bank account for you to use on something special." Mystery solved, now what are you going to do with the money? You could go out to dinner, or have a fun Friday night at the club; you could buy a new pair of shoes. You could also save it.

Now imagine that you have the same $100 increase in your bank account except it's not from Grandma. It is money you saved by cutting back on expenses recently. What would you do with this money? You have all the same options with the money. Yet somehow when I suggest that you save it, it sounds reasonable. When I suggested that you save Grandma's money, you thought I was being a killjoy.

Now I don't know enough about you and your life to make an intelligent recommendation on what to do with your slightly fatter wallet. However, I do know this. Your decision shouldn't be affected by whether that money came from grandma, extra hours at work, or cutbacks in your personal budget. Your bank account doesn't care where that money came from and neither should you.

There's a growing awareness in the area of personal financial planning that people often don't behave rationally with money. No kidding, right? Well up until about ten years ago or so, financial planners performed all of their analyses and presented all of their recommendations under the faulty assumption that people will act rationally with their money once they are educated about all of the benefits and consequences of their options on what to do with their money. The thinking goes "Once a person understands the issues, that person will certainly make the decision that benefits him the most."

Everyone in the real world, and now economists and financial planners as well, knows that people don't always act rationally with their money. There are many wonderful and peculiar quirks of human behavior that influence how we handle money. There is a growing science around this called Behavioral Economics. The story above exemplifies one finding in behavioral economics. Namely that the conditions leading to the receipt of an item affects how a person uses that item (even though it shouldn't).

OK, so as a result of this exercise you probably have reflected on your financial behavior in the past and realize that you too haven't always made the most rational decisions with regard to your own money. Now let me offer your first tool to help combat irrational money behavior you may consider in the future. Imagine different circumstances around how you got the money you are considering spending. Then decide: what you would with the money if those imagined circumstances were true. If the different circumstances you imagine result in you doing something different with your money, then spend some time justifying the different decisions to yourself. Whichever spending (or saving) decision has the best justification should be the decision you make. I find that when I think things through this way one decision is the clear winner.

Let me run through a new example. You got a $500 bonus at work. You are deciding what to do with the money. First, imagine what you would do if grandma sent you $500. Next, imagine what you would do if someone paid you $500 from your childhood collection of Pokémon cards that you are getting ready to throw out. Next, imagine what you would do if you got the bonus at work (which you did). Now justify what you would do with the money under each of those three scenarios. Doesn't one of your justifications stand head and shoulders above the rest? Well now you know the right thing to do with your $500.

This was the first of several thought experiments that I'll be sprinkling throughout my book series. These thought experiments are especially valuable because it is my observation that the biggest educational hurdle people must overcome in proper money management is in getting the education on how to avoid bad decisions with money that we would already know are bad decisions if we only took a moment to think about it.

# Chapter 9 - Introduction to Your Local Bank

I came up with this chapter title when I first prepared the outline to this book. Then I realized it was hard to make this chapter interesting with a title like that. Banks are supposed to be boring. You make deposits, you take money out by writing checks or going to the ATM. That's it.

Banking is the first step on the road to saving and building up a net worth. Ideally a person has their first relationship with a bank the first time they have enough money to not feel comfortable keeping their extra cash in their desk drawer. When this day happened for you, you probably strolled down to your local bank (they are all the same, right?), walked in with your first paycheck, or a wallet full of cash, handed over your money, filled out some forms, and became the owner of your first bank account. Most people, including me started banking this way. Most people made a mistake.

Your local bank is almost always the worst place to go to put your money. Your local bank is usually not local at all. It is usually a branch of a very large bank that has bank branches all across the country. These banks spend over a billion dollars a year (not an exaggeration) on advertising to convince you that they are your friend and partner in life and they would never take advantage of you. They get the money to pay for these ads by charging you bank fees.

Your budget for bank fees should be $0 per month; $0 per year; $0 per life. There is no excuse for bank fees. Paying a bank fee is like taking your money, lighting it on fire, and flushing it down the toilet. I don't understand why anyone would think it is a good deal to give a bank money and then pay the bank extra just to keep it safe. To me this sounds like a fee that the mob would think up– "Hey Joey, give me some money and I'll make sure nothing happens to this lovely savings account you have here. You know there are a lot of crooks out there, and you definitely need someone to protect your savings…"

Last week at my local bank branch[2] (one of the largest in America), I was unfortunate enough to hear an awful conversation between the woman ahead of me on line and the bank teller. The woman was concerned about her bank balance being much lower than she thought. The bank teller informed her that the bank charged an overdraft fee every time she was overdrawn on her checking account. This fee was "for her protection". The teller then explained to her that the "free" debit card that the bank gave her was

---

2 Yes I do have an account at a local bank. This bank is generally awful. However they provide free payroll services for my company. I am willing to deal with this awful bank in exchange for the payroll services. If the free payroll services went away, I would close the account and switch to an internet bank the same day.

attached to her checking account. Every time she uses it, it is equivalent to writing a check. If there isn't enough money in the account she is socked with a $10 overdraft fee. She was surprised that her account was ever overdrawn. She explained that her paycheck is direct deposited directly to her account. As the bank teller looked into her situation further, he informed her that when her account was opened, she was also given a "free" savings account. The bank set up the direct deposit to go to her savings account so she would benefit by having her money would be put to work right away. None of her income was put into her checking account that was charging her avoidable fees. Savings accounts at this bank currently earn 0.1% interest per year. That means that if she keeps an average of $2000 in her account, the bank will pay her about $0.17 cents a month in interest. For the final insult, the bank teller shared with her that last month alone, she had incurred $110 in overdraft fees. In short, her $0.17 in interest income from her savings account cost her $110 in fees on her checking account.

Please take this unfortunate experience as a cautionary tale. The existence of this woman's savings account was costing her $109.83 per month. That's an awful deal. For many people, a savings account is unnecessary, or even harmful. Even a high interest savings account will get you only about 1.0% interest per year. If you have $5000 saved, you are looking at just over $4 per month. One bank fee will wipe out all of your interest. Besides, you don't really want the hassle of having another bank account anyway.

I have never paid a bank fee in my life. A few times banks have put fees on my statement. Each time this happens, I go into the bank to complain about the fee, the teller explains they just sent a notice in the mail about a new reason to charge fees, I complain some more, and they reverse the charges "just once". Also, I do most of my banking at internet banks. They generally don't have any fees for anything, and they reimburse you for all of the ATM fees that other banks charge. The internet banks have the best ATM network in the country. You can use any ATM, anywhere, for free. Not even the largest bank in America can match that.

Having a bank account is simple. Keeping your bank from screwing you out of your money requires some knowhow and diligence. Look at your bank statement every month. The first red flag to look for are bank fees. Your budget for bank fees should be zero. There is no reason to ever pay a bank fee. There are plenty of banks out there that offer bank accounts with very low minimum balances. Credit unions and internet banks are good places to look for these accounts.

Key takeaways:

- The bank is not your friend.
- Savings accounts are generally not worth it.
- Paying a bank fee is like flushing money down the toilet.
- Your budget for bank fees should be $0.
- If a bank wants to charge you a fee, complain; if that doesn't work, close your account.
- Internet banks and credit unions are less likely to charge fees.

# Chapter 10 - Emergency Fund - What's the Point?

The point of an emergency fund is for emergencies, duh! Now some might say "I've got that covered, I'll use my credit card or I'll take out a loan for an emergency. Think about whether you think that is a smart, or even viable choice. You have an emergency, you don't have the money to fix it, and you take a $10,000 cash advance on your credit card and spend it to make the emergency go away.

Problem solved, temporarily. Now you've got a new, potentially worse problem. You just took out a 20% interest loan that won't pay down a cent until you've paid off the balance on your credit card from before the emergency. You've just taken on a $166.67 monthly interest charge for your cash advance. Even if you diligently pay the $166.67 on time every month, it will take you a long time to pay off this cash advance. How long? Forever! You see, the $166.67 payment is just your monthly interest charge. Paying that amount is just treading water, you've still got the $10,000 balance to contend with. If you up your payment to $200 per month, you will eventually pay off your emergency fund debt-- in 9 years! And face it, nobody's luck will run for 9 years in a row. You're going to have another emergency by then, and next time you won't be able to cash advance your way out of it.

How about the alternate solution of taking out a bank loan? That's not even viable. Here's how that plan is going to go "Hey Mr. X, thanks for your loan application, but it looks like you are under a bit of financial distress  and we aren't comfortable lending to you right now.  Give us a call after you've got your finances cleared up." You're not getting the loan. Nobody will lend to you if you are desperate.

So build an emergency fund. It'll be your best friend several times in your life. And maybe some times it will be your only friend. Start now with whatever money you have that you don't need to keep in your checking account to cover your bills this month.

Take this beginning of an emergency fund and give it its own secure home. Preferably in an online, no fee, high interest savings account.  Don't fill out the card to get a "free" ATM card. This will just lead to temptation. As a matter of fact if you get an ATM card anyway, cut it up and throw it out.  Commit to paying into your emergency fund every month just like any other bill. After all, your emergency fund is a bill. It is the bill for some future emergency you don't know about yet.

Pay 5% to 10% of your take home pay into your emergency fund. That's $200 a month for someone making $40K per year. This is very doable. If it isn't, consider cutting expenses somewhere else in life to make room for this payment. I guarantee your future emergency will be way more important than something you are spending $200 per month on now.

Now watch your emergency fund balance grow. The emergency fund bank statement should be very simple- a monthly deposit, some interest, and that's it. In a while you'll grow a solid emergency fund. My rule of thumb is that my emergency fund should be at least as big as how much I want to pay for my next car That's also a reason not to have your sights set on a brand new $30K SUV. If you are only putting away $200 a month, it'll take you over 12 years to build your emergency fund. Personally, I've never bought a new car, and I've never spent more than 2 month's salary on the used cars I've bought. Everyone is different, though. You decide a target emergency fund balance that works for you.

When you get there, hooray! This should help you sleep easier knowing that whatever happens, your emergency is taken care of. Now you can take your future emergency fund contributions and start down the road of investing.

## Chapter 11 - Investing 101 - Isn't That just Another Word for Saving?

We have to stay really high level here. After all there are entire books, textbooks even, on this subject. So this chapter is here to give you an initial knowledge that will give you the confidence to say "I can do this. I don't need to be rich to start investing. I don't need a financial advisor to start investing. I don't need a degree in finance to start investing. I can do this." Now that the goal of the chapter is laid out, let's get started.

First, investing is fundamentally different from saving. Saving is setting aside money because you expect to have a large expense / purchase sometime in the short to medium term. When you save money, the goal is to ensure that you have the money you need in the future. You don't expect your savings to change in value that much.

Investing is entirely different. The goal of investing is using your money to buy something that will make money for you. Investing involves risk-- when you purchase something that may make money for you, there is always a risk that the investment will fail and it will lose money. That's why you should never invest money that is needed for short term future expenses. Investing is OK for longer term expenses (5+ years in the future) because if your investment is unprofitable, you will have time to switch to a new investment that can recover your loss.

So you can start investing once you have enough saved for all your short- to mid- term expenses including an emergency fund, and a few thousand left over to meet the minimum investment requirements for many common investment opportunities. Let's say you're there. How do you start? Who do you call?

Who do you call? You call nobody! Anybody you call will be looking to earn a commission from an investment provider in exchange for convincing you to purchase that investment product. The commission may be a direct payment from you to the broker. Of course if you have to give money to a broker, you are able to invest less money and your investment will earn proportionately less.

Most people, even new investors, don't like the idea of giving up any of their investment dollars unless they have to. As a result, investment providers have an entire class of "no commission" products to attract stingy people like you and me.  Did you notice that "no commission" is in quotes? That's because these products aren't really no commission products, they are hidden commission products. Investment providers are allowed to deduct investment expenses directly from your investments. Typical expenses include administrative overhead, advertising, the salary of the investment team managing your investment, etc. In addition, some investment include a "trailing commission" as an expense. This is a commission that the investment provider will pay to your broker every year you are still holding the investment he recommended to you. The investment provider pays the commission with your money. The broker will still get this commission even if he never speaks to you again after your initial purchase. Talk about money for nothing! Some investments actually provide brokers with both types of commissions. No wonder brokers are so interested in talking to you.

Let's see how this works with a detailed example:

January 1 you invest $10,000 in a no load stock fund that has a hidden commission. The stocks in this fund increase in value by 10%. Your share of the stocks in this fund are now worth $11,000. The expense ratio for your fund is 1.0%. This means that your share of the expenses of the fund is $110 ($11,000 x 1% = $110). Your mutual fund company uses that money to pay their investment advisors and other investment expenses. Your mutual fund company also uses that money to pay a trailing commission to the broker who got you to purchase the fund. Your mutual fund then sends you a statement saying that your fund is now worth $10,890 ($11,000 - $110 = $10,890). The broker who you haven't spoke to in over a year quietly cashes his commission check. In later chapters I will show you how to identify which mutual funds do and don't have a trailing commission.

The best way to get started investing is to go online where so many things are free. Your first investment should be easy to understand, simple, of moderate risk level and of course, low expense. I just described all of the features of an index mutual fund.

An index fund is a fund that combines your investment with all the other investments in the fund. The fund manager then takes this money and buys all of the stocks in that index. You share all of the dividends of those stocks, and when you sell your index fund at some time in the distant future, the value of your fund will have increased by the same percentage as the index. Historically stock indices have doubled every 7 to 10 years. Yes, there's an expense ratio, but it is tiny. Vanguard has an index fund for entry level investors that charges only $1.70 per year for every $1,000 you invest (less than the price of a Coke). That's an awesome deal. There are other mutual fund companies that offer similarly priced index funds. A low cost index fund is the best way to begin investing for the long term.

# Chapter 12 - Mutual Funds

Mutual funds are the best first investment. As a matter of fact, unless you have special skill with a particular type of investment, most of your investment dollars should be placed in mutual funds no matter how long you've been investing. Mutual funds cost money, some are expensive, some are very risky, and some have had lousy returns. All that being said, if you know what you are doing you can find an inexpensive mutual fund designed to deliver for you.

I looked online to see what definitions of mutual funds are available and I found every single definition confusing. Most of the definitions imply that mutual funds are doing something way more complicated than they really are. Mutual funds are actually quite simple. A mutual fund accepts deposits from many investors, and makes investments with the money. In return, investors get shares of the mutual fund. Each share costs the same amount of money, so the more money you deposit into the fund, the more shares you get.

 Each mutual fund has a manager that decides when to buy and sell investments for the fund. When investments earn interest or dividends, the money is deposited in the fund, The fund manager uses money from the fund to pay all of the fund's expenses (e.g. salary of the manager, commissions to brokers, investment research reports, etc.). At the end of each trading day, the mutual fund adds up the value of all of the stocks, bonds, bank accounts and other investments of the fund and divides that value by the number of shares. This is the share price at the end of the day. Whenever you want, you can sell your shares back to the mutual fund. The mutual fund will pay you that day's share price.

You don't get to vote on the investment decisions of the mutual fund. The investment manager has sole discretion over those decisions. However all mutual funds have a written description detailing the types of investments they make. For example, here's part of the description of one mutual fund I am looking at:

" A low cost way to gain diversified exposure to the U.S. equity market. The fund invests in 500 of the largest U.S. companies, which span many different industries and account for about three-fourths of the U.S. stock market's value ..."

This fund is a S&P 500 index fund. Many fund companies have this type of fund. It's a good choice for someone who wants exposure to the stock market.

# Chapter 13 - How to Select a Mutual Fund

It is generally easier to pick a good index fund and index funds perform just as well as actively managed funds. So I recommend an index fund as your first mutual fund. First, what is an index fund? An index fund is a mutual fund that is designed to perform the same as a particular stock index. For example, the description at the end of the last chapter is for a S&P500 index fund. Index funds have lower expenses because they don't have an investment manager that needs to buy a new yacht every year. All an index fund needs is a computer program that buys stocks in the S&P500 index. You can find companies offering index funds with expenses of less than 0.2% per year. Contrast that expense ratio to the expense ratio of an actively managed fund around 1.2%. That actively managed fund must do 1.0% better than the stock market index every year just to stay even. It's really hard for an investment manager to beat the stock indexes by more than 1.0% consistently. It's even harder for an investor to identify the investment managers that are going to beat the stock indexes next year. For these reasons, I suggest that everyone sticks with an index fund.

Index funds are basically a commodity. You don't really care what mutual fund company's computer program is investing in the index for you. It's all the same. So when selecting an index fund price is most important. And, as discussed earlier, the price you pay for a fund is revealed in the fund's expense ratio.

So now is the time to go online and let your fingers do the walking. Type "low cost S&P500 index fund" into your favorite search engine. You should see results from all of the big no-load firms such as Vanguard, Fidelity, Schwab, and a few others. Go to each of these sites and click on the link for the S&P500 index fund. Read all the information, but most importantly look for a chart that states what the expense ratio for the fund is. Lower is better. Pick the lowest. Make sure again there are no sales charges (The companies I mention above have none.) Fill out the online form. Mail in your check. Congratulations, you are an investor! And more importantly, you are now investing in something you understand.

## Chapter 14 - Conclusion

I hope you enjoyed the book. With this book you have a solid foundation on how to think about money. Upon completing this book, your fear and anxiety around personal money issues should be shrinking, and your preparedness around money issues should be growing. This book was an important first step towards your goal of never making an uninformed financial decision again.

The second book is titled Starting to Make Money. The goal of this book is to get you thinking about everyday money issues that everyone faces. You will learn about car loans, everyday spending and saving decisions. and money issues affecting your social life. This book takes the personal finance foundation developed in book one and applies it to the real world. After reading this book you'll be comfortable effectively managing your personal budget. You'll be generating positive cash flow in your life and will be starting down a path that will lead to traditional investing and wealth building.

The third book is titled An Adult Relationship with Money. This book is where most personal finance books start. To me, starting an understanding of personal finance with this book is kind of like starting to build a house on the third floor, or teaching algebra before multiplication. There's no way you can be successful in managing your taxes, investments, loans, and financial advisers until you have the foundation contained in the first two books. This third book is the book most similar to traditional personal finance books. You'll understand this book more though, because this book series gives you the foundation of financial knowledge  necessary to understand personal finance. The knowledge you gather in this book will likely guide you to financial decisions in the near future that improve your finances by a few thousand dollars per year compared to the poor financial decisions you might have made without this book.

The fourth book is titled Now You Have Money. This book discusses financial issues and decisions you'll face if you follow the guidance in the first three books. It discusses retirement investing, annuities, and other issues related to managing a six or seven figure net work. If you're not in that wealth category yet, you will be soon enough. Just follow the guidance from the first three books. It's great to be ahead of the game and have the peace of mind knowing how to handle your future wealth before you actually have it.

The fifth and final book is titled Extra Credit - Money for Fun. This book is the final step of the personal finance journey. Among other things it discusses personal finance issues around being set for life and keeping yourself educated about  personal finance. If you're not set for life yet, don't fret. Just follow the guidance in the first four books and be patient. You'll make it.  Think of this book as the "continuing ed" book on personal finance.

I welcome all feedback. Feel free to contact me at Hayden@ForwardFinancialPlanners.com. This is your gateway to share one-off commentary, suggestions for future books, or to get on the distribution list for updates related to future publication.

You can also subscribe to www.TypeZFinance.com for my weekly thoughts on  personal finance issues that have caught my attention.

www.ingramcontent.com/pod-product-compliance
Lightning Source LLC
Chambersburg PA
CBHW071327200326
41520CB00013B/2888